The Fastest Way to Improve at Chess

A
Thinking System
to Find Better Moves

By

James Demery

For Diana, Harold and Michael and everyone in my family. Many thanks to my friend Bob, without whom this book would not be possible. For Ronnie who left us too soon. God rest his soul.

I love chess. I love its symmetry and its logic. I just wasn`t very good at it. At least not as good as I thought. So, I resigned myself to reading about great chess players of the past and present. If I couldn`t play great chess myself at least I could read and play through the games of great players that could play great chess.

One day I ran into an old friend I hadn`t seen in years. We started talking and my friend Bob and I agreed to start meeting once a week to play chess. Eventually I became disappointed in my level of play, so I decided to put together a study plan to improve.

I decided I should start with improving my Opening basics, Endgame basics, Tactics and developing a workable Thinking System.

The Opening

My approach to the Opening had been to develop my pieces, Castle, and figure things out as I went along. Often, I would get a reasonable position, but sometimes I would get in a lot of trouble and I was constantly using too much time on the clock.

I wanted to primarily play 1 e4 and occasionally 1 f4 just for a change of pace. I thought about the Openings I would have to face with White and Black and came up with the following list of the Openings I would face most often:

White vs e5, e6, c5, c6, d5, d6, Nf6, Nc6, g6 and b6.

Black vs e4, c4, f4, Queen`s Gambit, London, Veresov, Colle, King`s Indian Attack and Catalan.

I decided to assemble and play through games of Master level players and see how GM`s played these Openings and to see particularly where they placed their pieces. Several great writers (I`m talking about great writers, unlike me) recommend going over GM games to improve.

In addition to GM games I also decided I would assemble games that I would play against the computer and see how it attacked these Openings. For example, to see how the computer would attack the Sicilian, I would play the Sicilian against the computer and see how it responded. I reasoned that since I was below Master level, and any opponents I would face were also, their moves would be approximately the same as mine. I printed these games out and created a catalog of games against these Openings.

The Endgame

To address my problems in the Endgame I decided I needed to start with learning the Basic Endings. I started with a book called 100 Endgames You Must Know by Jesus de la Villa. The author has assembled the 100 most common Endings and I decided to put the positions in my phone. There are well over 100 examples of these positions in the book and having them on my phone made them easier to study. I also got a notebook and made brief notes of each position so that I could quickly go through the problems during my study time. If you go through 20 problems a day you can work through all the problems in a week.

Tactics

My next challenge was Tactics. I thought I was ok at Tactics, but when I would review my games with the computer I would invariably see things that I had missed. As I was trying to come up with a way to address this I remembered a book review from several years ago by Jeremy Silman.

The book was Rapid Chess Improvement, and everyone agreed that solving Tactics problems was very important. The problem is his program was unworkable for me. His program calls for you to spend several hours a day solving Tactics problems. I`d love to stay home from work and solve Tactics problems all day, but I was afraid if I did my wife would come after me with a rolling pin.

I did learn from all the articles and controversy at the time that solving Tactics problems and learning as many patterns as I could was the best way to improve at Tactics and reduce the oversights I was having. I put a few hundred problems on my phone and I also began solving problems on a couple of different websites online.

.

Thinking System

A lot of times during a chess game I would find that with the clock running I would look at the position and make a move that seemed to meet the needs of the situation, but I didn`t really have a systematic method of thinking or choosing moves. By culling different articles and a lot of trial and error (mostly error) I assembled the following list of guidelines:

1 Move attack / unprotect

2 Checks and captures

3 Undefended pieces

4 What`s attacking / defending what

5 Attack every piece

6 Pins

7 Best piece placement

8 Moves where pieces contact

I wrote this down on a piece of paper and keep this by my computer while I`m solving Tactics problems. You can also keep it by your computer when you`re playing games online and get in the habit of glancing at it after each move. Let`s look at each and then see them in a game situation.

1 Move attack / unprotect

Naturally you want to look and see what your opponent`s move is attacking and determine if you need to respond or if you can ignore the threat.

We also need to note if our opponent`s move has left a piece or a key square unprotected. I can`t tell you how many good moves I`ve missed because I didn`t notice what my opponent`s move had weakened. Of course, before we make a move we need to be aware of what we`re weakening. I`ve fallen into some brutal attacks by being so focused on what I wanted to attack that I didn`t notice some weakness I was creating. Try to remember the old saying that your opponent has a right to exist too.

2 Checks and captures

Many articles have been written by many great writers that have taught us the importance of looking at every check and every capture and I`m sure most of us have tried to do this. We must look very carefully no matter how outlandish it looks. It may look like capturing a pawn with your Queen is suicidal, but when your opponent recaptures it may open a diagonal that proves fatal to your opponent`s King.

3 Undefended pieces

Many articles have also been written that talk about the importance of looking to see if any of our opponent`s pieces are undefended because of the possibility of undertaking operations against them. Always identify any undefended pieces, especially your own.

4 What`s attacking / defending what

This is a very important step because it`s here that we determine exactly what each piece and pawn is doing. We can`t devise a plan until we know what the pieces are up to and what they control. When I`m trying to solve Tactics problems I start with my opponent`s pieces in the top left corner and move left to right and identify what each piece and pawn is doing. Then I do the same with my pieces and pawns.

In an actual game you will want to start from move one, making a mental note with each move what function the move is performing and the strengths and weaknesses you`re creating.

5 Attack every piece

With this step we want to look and see if there is some way we can launch an attack on each of our opponent`s pieces. By now you`re probably thinking "This is your suggestion to find better moves...attack my opponent`s pieces?" Well, yes. You must have a plan of course, but you want to be flexible. We want to see if the opponent`s pieces are vulnerable, and if they are, we may find a better plan. Starting with the Queen, then the Rooks, then the minor pieces and then the pawns see if there is some way of undertaking an attack against any of these units. It will also help you reduce mistakes because you will automatically learn more about your opponent`s capabilities which will lead to fewer oversights.

6 Pins

We all know what Pins are and many people have written about the benefits of being able to attack a pinned piece. Always note when there are pinned pieces on the board.

7 Best piece placement

Always be careful to focus on the piece placement of your pieces and those of your opponent. Try always to improve your pieces and hinder your opponent`s ability to do the same. Bobby Fischer almost always had better piece placement than his opponents and when he did have a poorly placed piece he would improve it or trade it off.

8 Moves where pieces contact

I don`t remember where I read this. I think it was an article on Chess.com, but I can`t remember who wrote it. I don`t mean to not credit someone because I would like to give credit to the person that taught me this important insight. The gist of it was to always be aware of any move by you or your opponent that would bring pieces or pawns into contact. By being aware of this you will find that you will have fewer tactical oversights.

Game Positions

Let`s see how this system works in an actual game. This position arose from the Bird Opening. I prefer 1e4, but my buddy Bob likes to play the Bird Opening so I played his opening against him just to see his reaction and we arrived at this position.

1 Move attack / unprotect

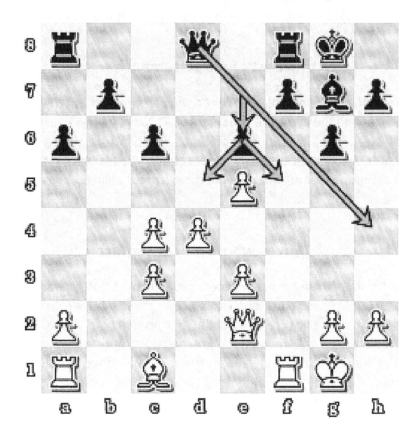

I have more space in the center, doubled pawns on the Queenside and the half open f file. The Kingside looks like the best side for me to operate. My opponent has connected pawns on the Queenside and I think better prospects there. He played 14 ...e6 weakening d6 and f6, strengthening d5 and f5, preventing Whites pawn on e5 from advancing and opening the d8-h4 diagonal for his Queen.

2 Checks and captures

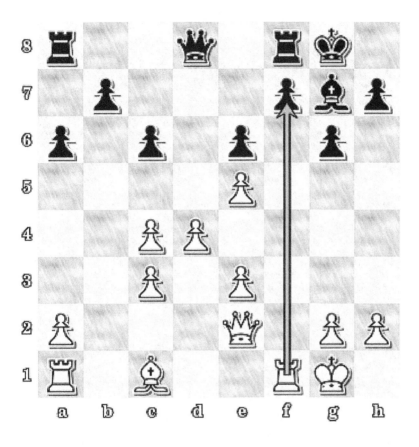

I don`t see a way to Check either King for several moves and the only capture I see is Rxf7 which is unviable, but you always want to note the capture.

3 Undefended pieces

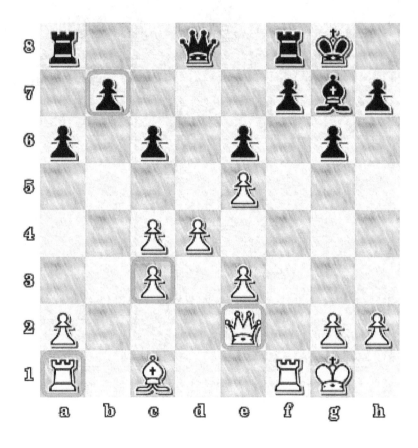

Black`s b7 pawn, White`s a1 Rook, c3 pawn and White`s Queen on e2 are undefended.

4 What`s attacking / defending what

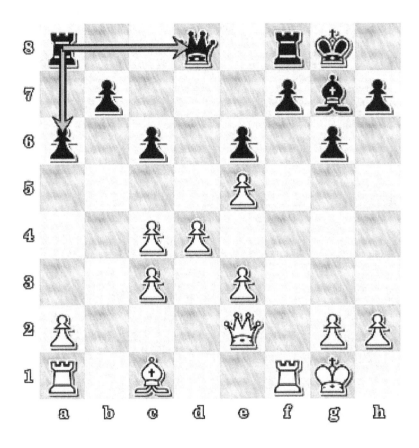

Starting in the top left corner the a8 Rook is defending the a file, the back rank squares and the Queen.

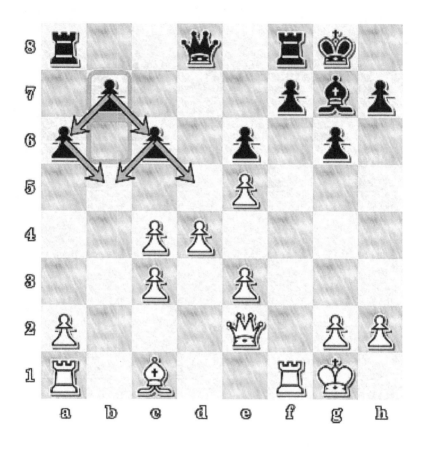

Of the Queenside pawns the b7 pawn is undefended and is protecting the a6 and c6 pawns which are protecting b5 and d5. The b6 square is weak.

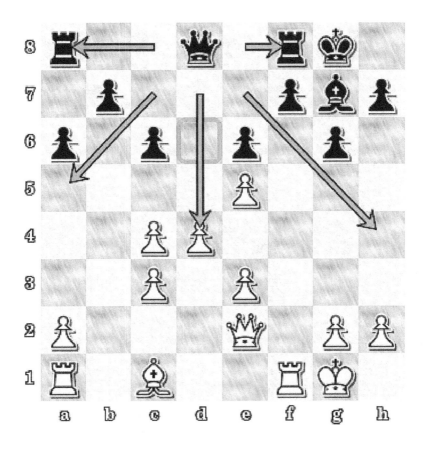

The Queen is attacking the pawn on d4, protecting both Rooks, strengthening the d8-a5 and d8-h4 diagonals and the d file. The d6 square is weak.

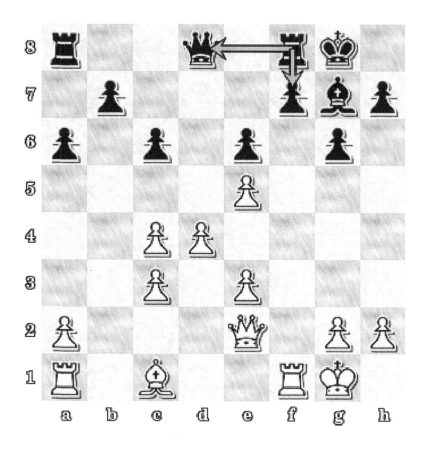

The f8 Rook has not been moved since Castling and is defending the Queen and f7 pawn.

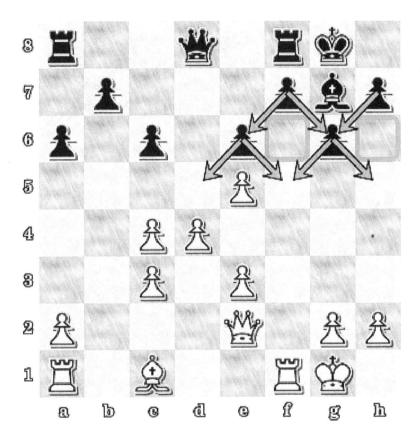

The Kingside pawns are protecting d5, e6, f5, g6, and h5. The f6 and h6 squares are weak.

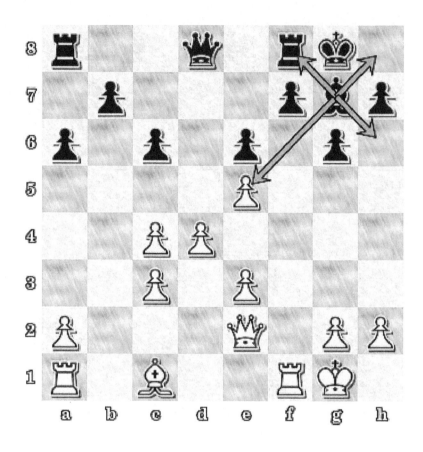

The g7 Bishop is attacking e5 on the h8-f1 diagonal, protecting the Rook and defending f6, h6 and h8.

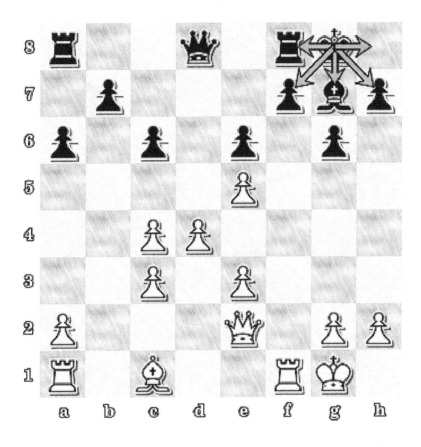

The King is protecting the f8 Rook, g7 Bishop, the f7, h7 pawns and the h8 square.

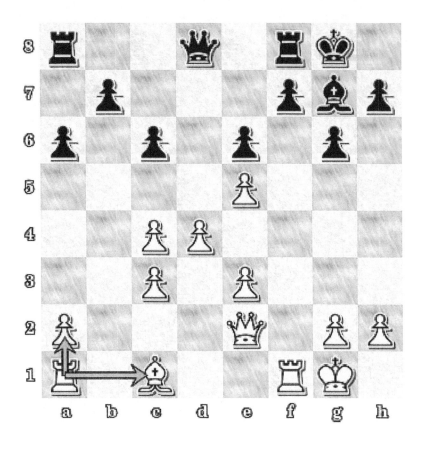

Now my pieces. The a1 Rook is defending the a2 pawn, the b1 square and the c1 Bishop.

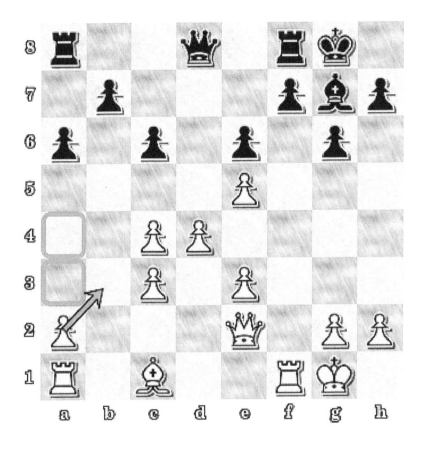

The a2 pawn is defending b3 and the a3 and a4 squares are weak.

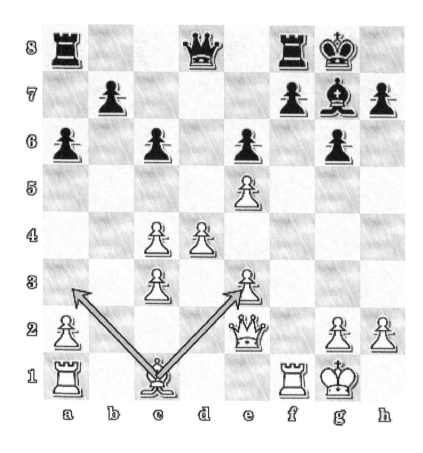

The Bishop is strengthening the c1-a3 and c1-h6 diagonals and defending the e3 pawn.

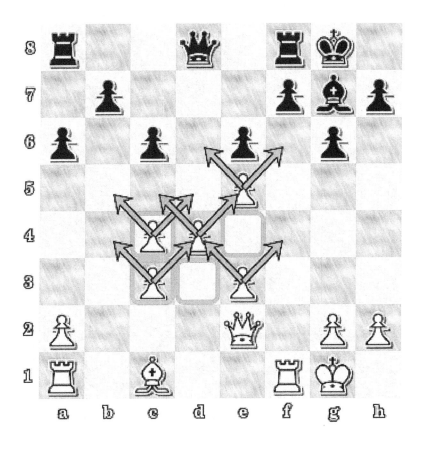

The mass of pawns in the center are defending b4, b5, c5, d5, d4, e5, d6, f6 and f4. The c3, c4, d3 and e4 squares are weak.

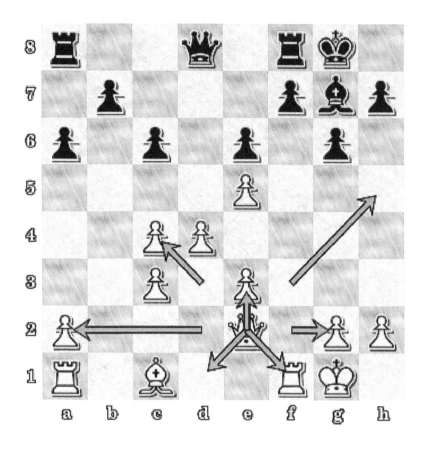

The Queen on e2 is strengthening the e file, the 2nd rank, the f1-a6 and d1-h5 diagonals, and the f1 Rook.

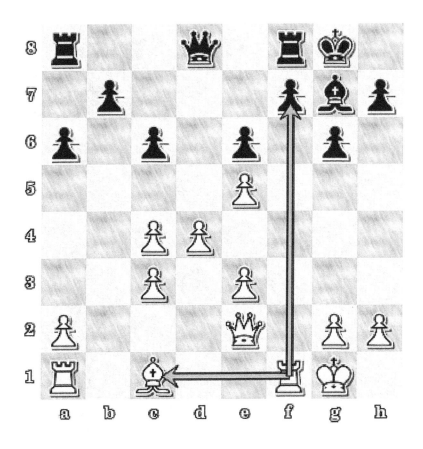

The f1 Rook is strengthening the back rank, the f file, protecting the c1 Bishop and attacking f7.

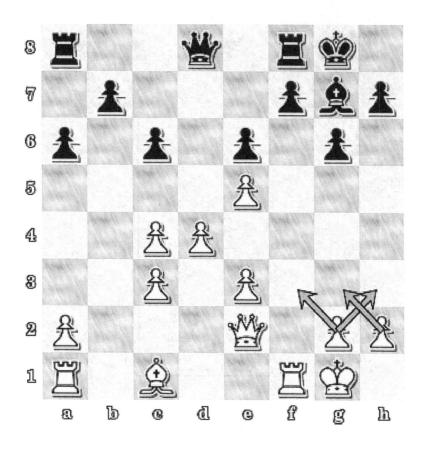

The 2 Kingside pawns are defending f3, g3, and h3.

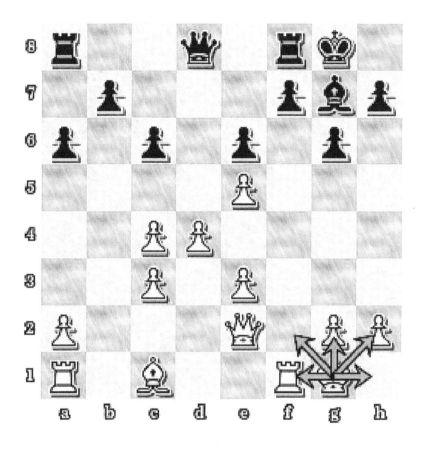

The King is protecting the Rook as well as f2, g2, h2 and h1.

From here on we will update this as we go along. Since we picked this up in the middlegame we had to identify what was going on. In your games you will want to identify what each move is doing from move 1 and do this breakdown when solving Tactics problems.

5 Attack every piece

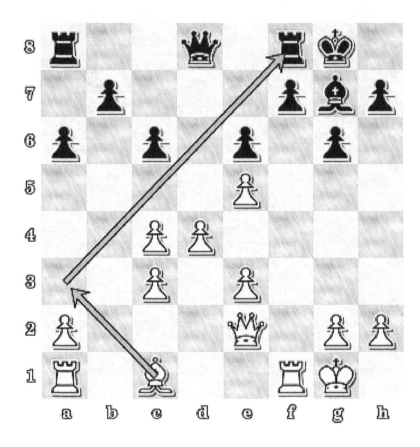

The only piece that can be attacked is the Rook on f8. We identified the pawn on f7 earlier. It will take several moves to attack any other pieces.

6 Pins

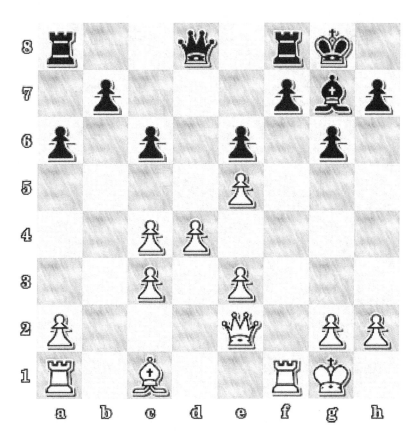

I don`t see any pins to exploit.

7 Best piece placement

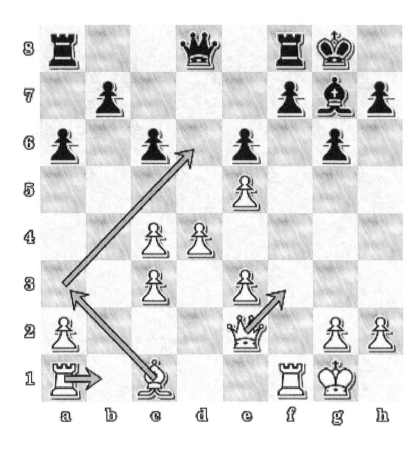

My Bishop, Queen and a1 Rook are poorly placed. I want to get my Bishop to the d6 outpost, centralize my Queen and get my a1 Rook to b1 or, at some point, to double up on the f file.

8 Moves pieces contact

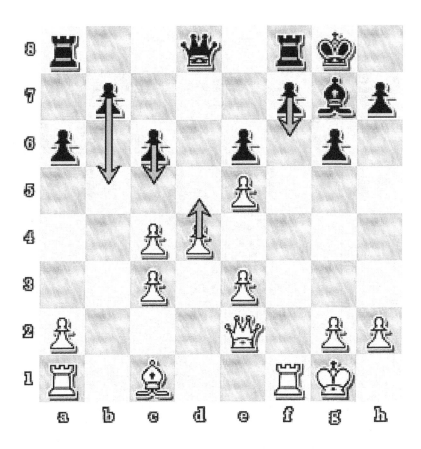

I see d5 for White and b5, c5 and f6 for black.

At first these steps look cumbersome and time consuming, but with practice you can do this quickly and I have less time trouble than I had before.

15 Ba3

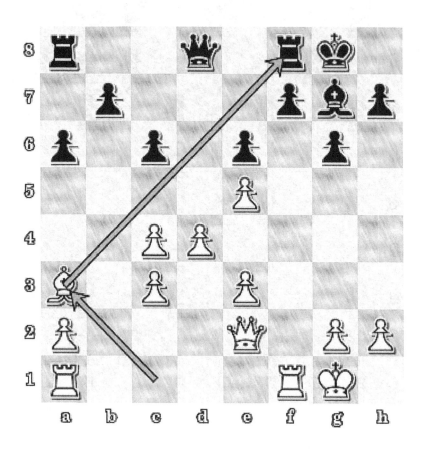

Weakening the c1-h6 diagonal, strengthening the a3-f8 diagonal, attacking the f8 Rook and removing a defender from the e3 pawn.

15 ...Re8

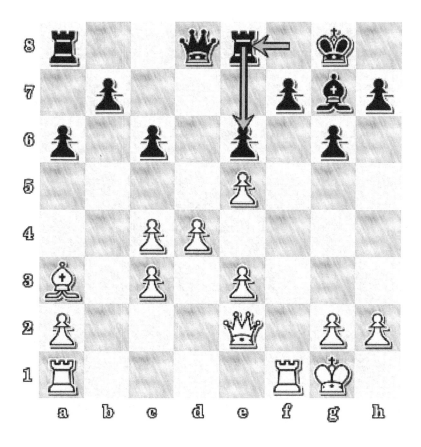

Weakening the f file, strengthening the e file and removing a defender from the f7 pawn.

16 Qf3

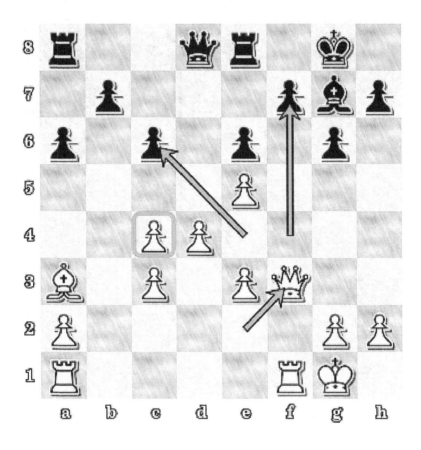

Weakening the 2nd rank, the f1-a6 diagonal, the e file and leaving the c4 pawn unprotected strengthening the 3rd rank, the f file, the h1-a8 diagonal and attacking f7 and c6.

16...Qd7

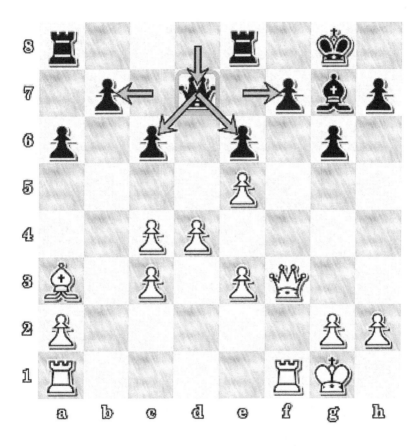

Weakening the back rank and the d8-a5 and d8-h4 diagonals, strengthening the 7th rank and the c6, and e6 pawns, and defending the f7 pawn. The Queen is undefended.

17 Bd6

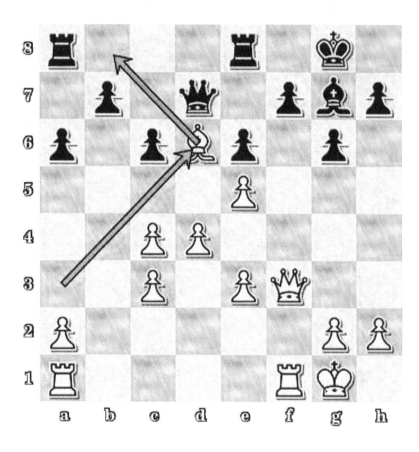

Weakening the c1-a3 diagonal, strengthening c7 and b8 and obtaining the outpost we identified in Step 7.

17 ...b5

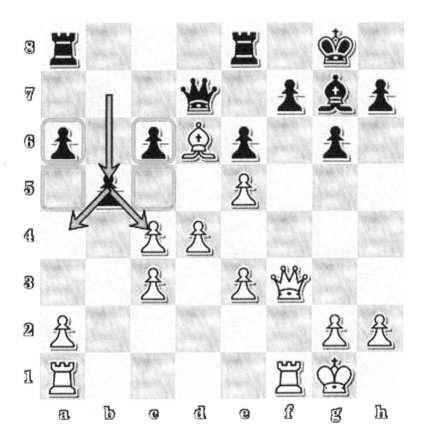

Weakening a6, a5, c6 and c5, strengthening a4 and attacking the c4 pawn. This was one of the moves we identified earlier in Step 8. Let`s look at the position now using our list.

1 Move attack / unprotect

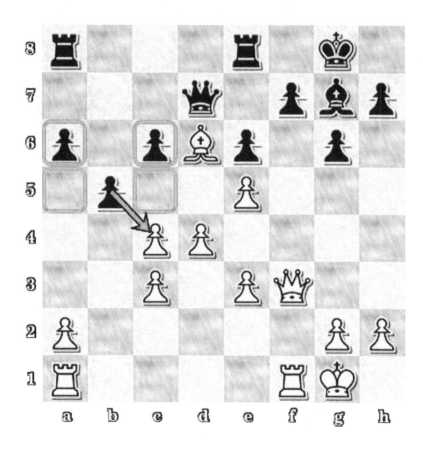

He`s attacking the c4 pawn and weakened the squares we just identified.

2 Checks and captures

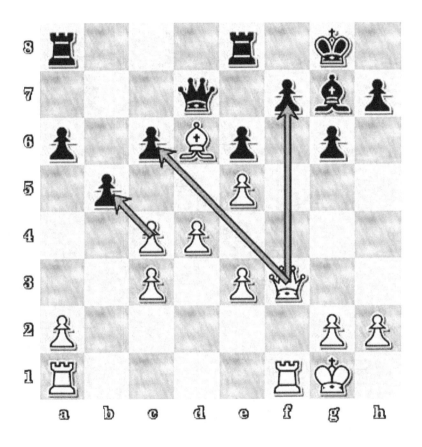

The checks and captures on f7 and c5 are unviable. Another capture is cxb5, but I would rather play c5 and add another defender to my Bishop.

3 Undefended pieces

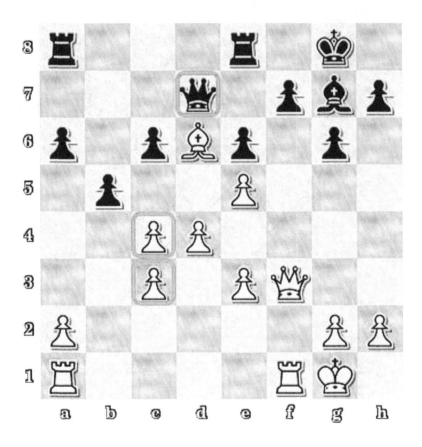

The c3 and c4 pawns and Queen on d7 are unprotected. 4 What's attacking / defending what We've updated this as we've gone along.

5 Attack every piece

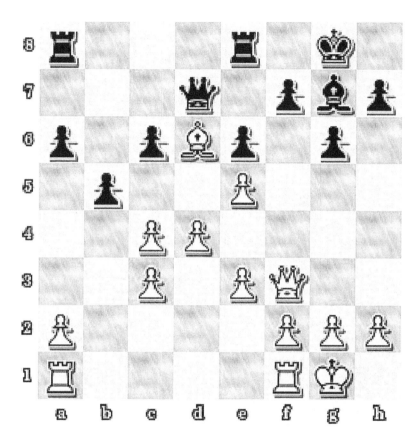

It's still difficult to mount an attack on any of his pieces in the next few moves. The Queen on d7 is unprotected and that's one of the signs we look for to see if a piece is vulnerable but she's so far behind enemy lines it's hard to get to her. 6 Pins - I don't see any pins that can be taken advantage of.

7 Best piece placement

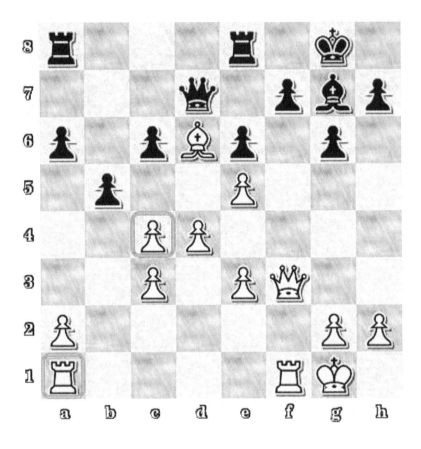

I still haven`t managed to improve my Rook on a1, but before I get to that I have to deal with my pawn on c4.

8 Moves pieces contact

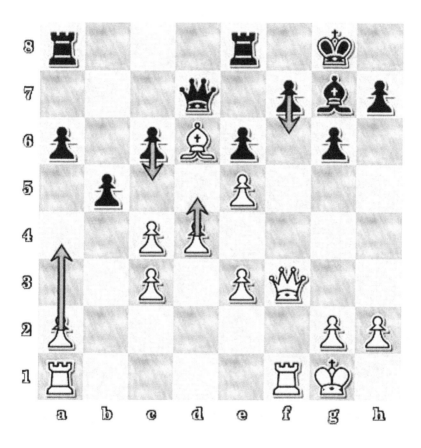

The pawn moves a4 and d5 both create contact with other units, but neither move is good for me. My opponent has c5 and f6.

18 c5

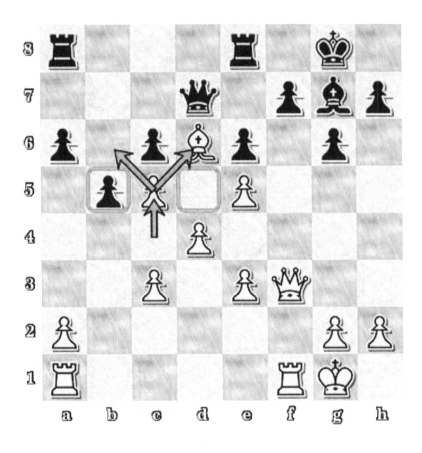

Weakening b5 and d5, strengthening b6 and d6 and adding another defender to the d6 Bishop.

18 ...Bf8

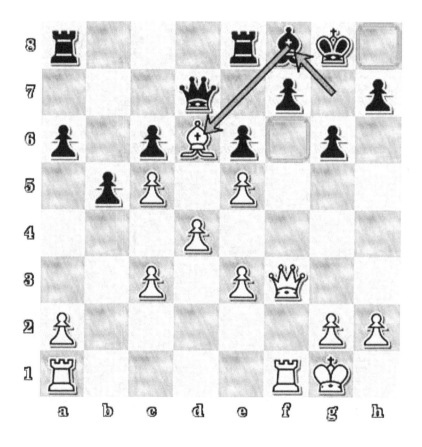

Weakening the h8-a1 diagonal, the f6 and h8 squares, strengthening the f8-a3 diagonal and attacking the d6 Bishop.

19 Qf6

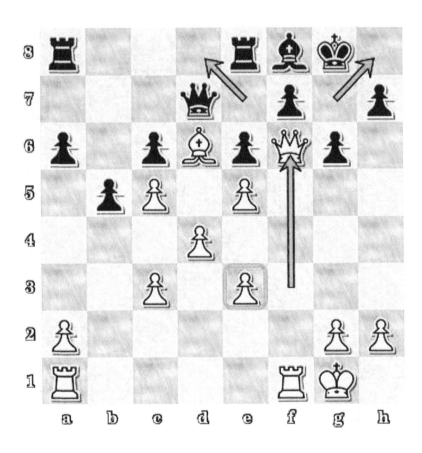

Weakening the 3rd rank, the d1-h5 and h1-a8 diagonals, leaving e3 unprotected, strengthening the 6th rank, the a1-h8 and h4-d8 diagonals and keeping the pawn on f7 from moving forward.

19 ...Bg7

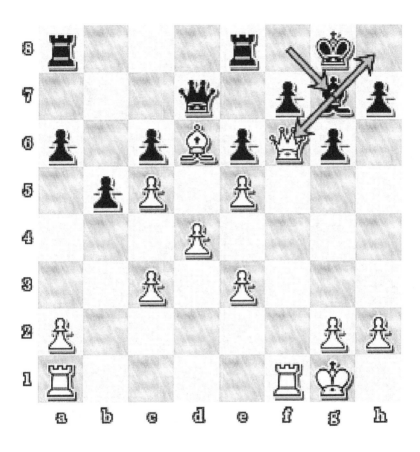

Weakening the f8-a3 diagonal, strengthening the h8-a1 diagonal, the h8 square and attacking the Queen. He didn't want to trade Bishops and have a passed pawn that far up the board to blockade and having your opponent's Queen close to your King is never good.

20 Qf3

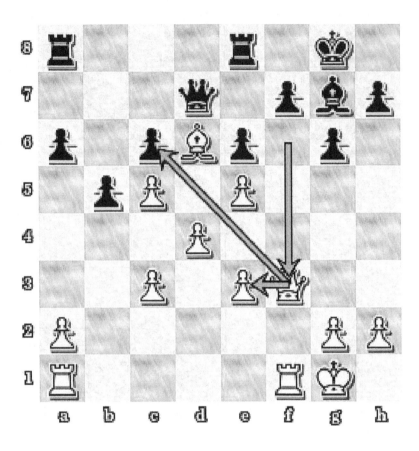

Moving the Queen off the a1-h8 and h4-d8 diagonals and back onto the d1-h5 and h1-a8 diagonals, protecting e3 and resuming the attack on c6. What I wanted most to do is advance my Queen, double my Rooks on the f file, start advancing the h pawn and attack on the Kingside. My opponent can transfer his forces to the Queenside and start operations over there which is, in fact what he did.

20 ...Ra7

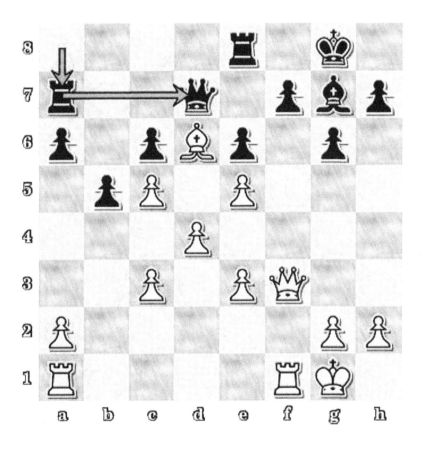

Weakening the back rank, strengthening the 7th rank defending the Queen. Now my opponent can put his a7 Rook on b7, then his e8 Rook on a8 and start his Queenside attack.

21 a3

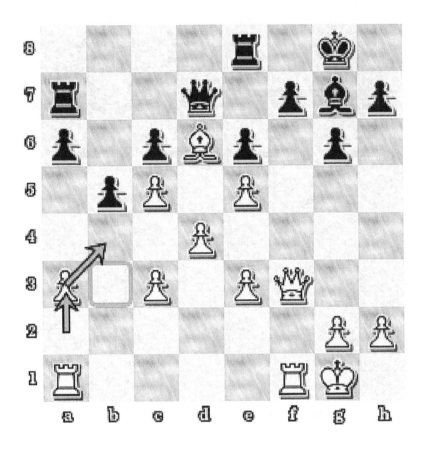

Weakening b3 and strengthening the b4 square. I hadn't forgotten about my Kingside plans, but by now I had 24 minutes on the clock and my opponent had less than 10 minutes. Let's not just give up the Queenside, transfer to the Kingside and play race to the King. I wanted to contest that side of the board and make my opponent keep finding moves and using his time. I have a solid position and if I don't do anything stupid I should be fine.

21 ...Rb7

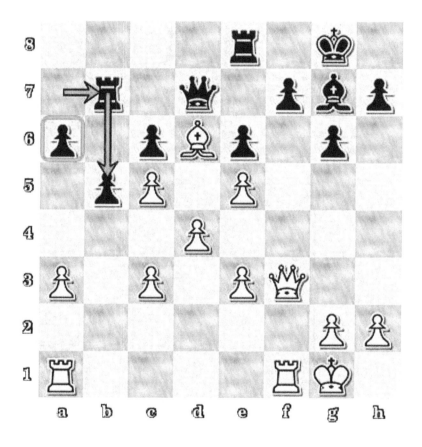

Weakening the a file leaving a6 unprotected and strengthening the b file. I think his best hope is still to expand on the Queenside and try to achieve a breakthrough there.

22 Rab1

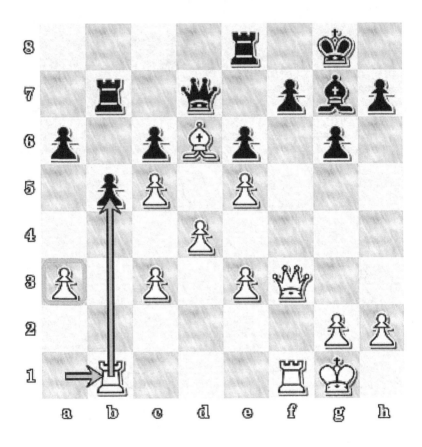

Weakening, the a file leaving a3 unprotected and strengthening the b file. Still contesting the Queenside. I still want to be prepared to transfer my attack to the Kingside.

22 ...Ra8

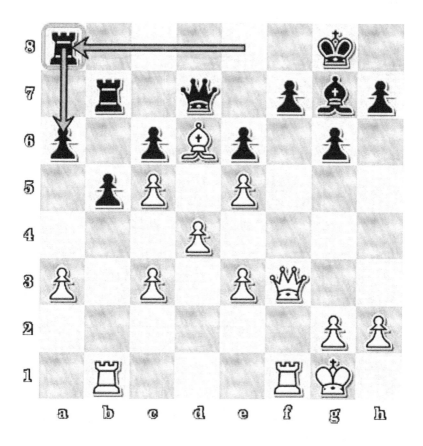

Weakening the e file and strengthening the a file. The a8 Rook is unprotected. Again, we anticipated this move as he continues building up on the Queenside.

23 Rb2

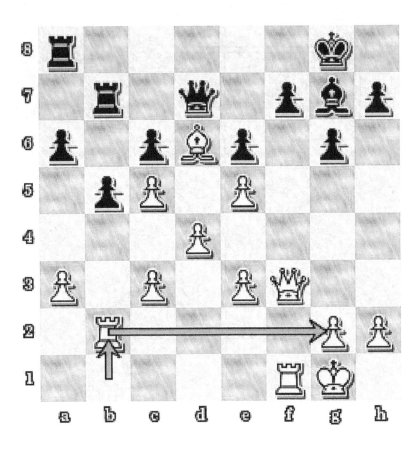

Weakening the back rank and strengthening the 2nd rank. I did this so that I could double the Rooks on the b file to help me contest the Queenside or, if needed, on the f file to attack on the Kingside.

23 ...Qd8

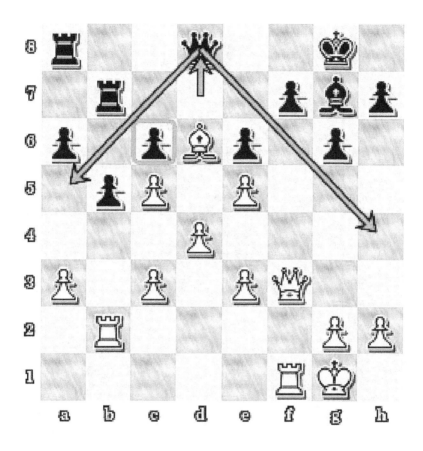

Weakening the c8-h3 and e8-a4 diagonals, the 7th rank, strengthening the back rank and d8-a5 and d8-h4 diagonals. Making a mistake I`ve made countless times. He wanted to move his Queen to a5 to help on the Queenside, but in repositioning his Queen he left the c6 pawn unprotected. In his defense time his time was becoming critical. He had less than 8 minutes on the clock while I had 23 minutes.

24 Qxc6

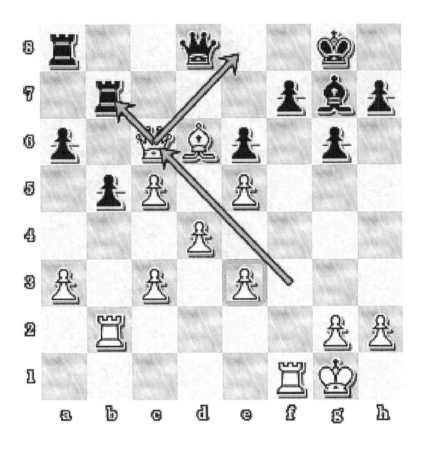

Weakening the f file, the 3rd rank and d1-h5 diagonal leaving e3 unprotected, strengthening the c file, the 6th rank the a4-e8 diagonal, capturing the c6 pawn, creates a passed pawn on c5 and attacks the Rook on b7.

24 ...Raa7

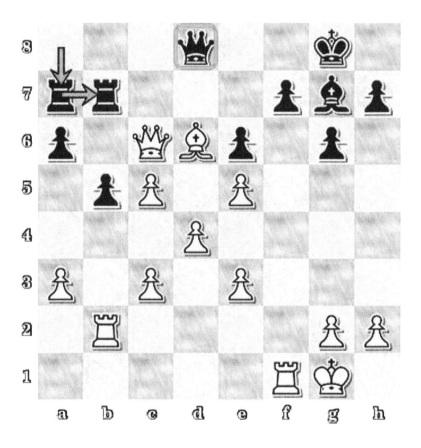

Weakening the back rank leaving the Queen unprotected and protects the Rook on b7.

25 Qf3

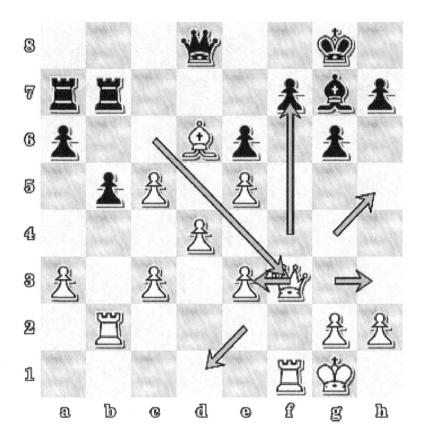

Weakening the c file, the 6th rank and the a4-e8 diagonal, strengthening the f file the 3rd rank, and the d1-h5 diagonal, protecting e3, and moving the Queen so the c5 pawn can advance.

25 ...Qa5

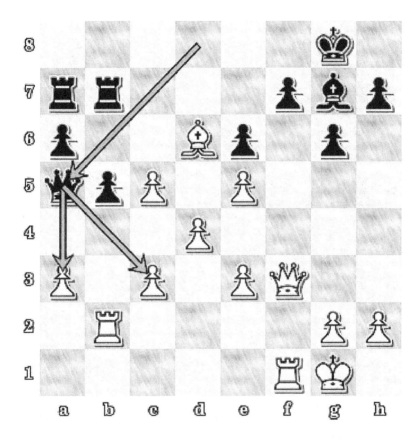

Weakening the d file, the back rank and d8-h4 diagonal, strengthening, the a file, b5 pawn, the e1-h5 diagonal and attacking the a3 and c3 pawns.

26 Rb3

Weakens the 2nd rank and protects a3 and c3. I wanted to slow down his counter play on the Queenside and then push the c pawn. I could have played c6, but I wanted to keep him thinking and not give him any obvious captures like Qxa3 or Qxc3.

26 ...Qa4

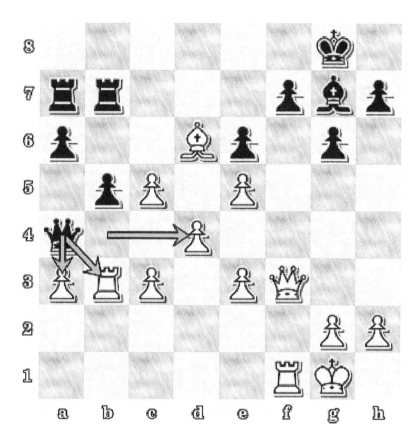

Weakening the d8-a5 and a5-e1 diagonals, the 5th rank, strengthening the 4th rank and attacking the d4 pawn and the b3 Rook.

27 c6

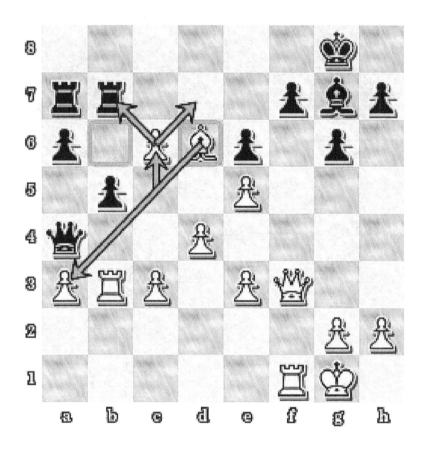

Weakening b6 and d6, strengthening the f8-a3 diagonal, d7, and attacking the b7 Rook. I thought about doubling the Rooks on the b file, but I decided to ignore his threat and make one of my own. If he takes my b3 Rook, I`ll take his b7 Rook and he must give up his a7 Rook to keep the pawn from promoting.

27 ...Rb6

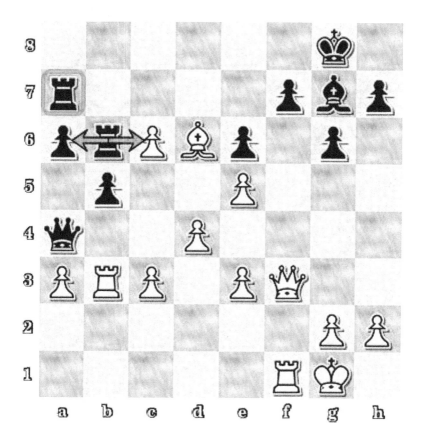

Weakening the 7th rank leaving the Rook on a7 unprotected, strengthening the 6th rank and attacking the pawn on c6.

28 c7

Weakening b7 and d7, strengthening b8 and d8 and is one square from promoting. I thought here he must give up the Rook to stop the pawn, but my opponent had very little time on the clock to work out a defense.

28 ...Rab7 29 c8=Q+ 29 ...Bf8 30 Qxf8#.

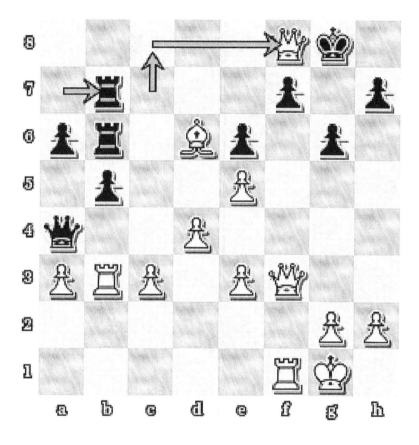

By using the list and updating these steps along the way I was able to formulate plans and place my pieces well. I was disappointed with 19 Qf6 which cost me time and wasn't the greatest move of our age, but it wasn't a game ending blunder. I encourage you to set up a chessboard and play through this game and chess games you have played while going over these steps.

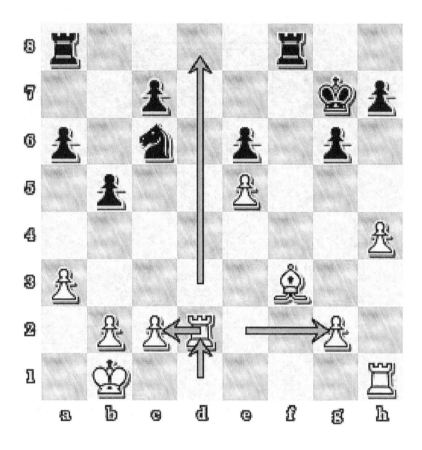

Let's look at another game. This position arose from the Pirc Defense. Black has more space on the Queenside, White the center and on the Kingside. In the center Black has an isolated pawn on e6 that I want to target. Let's use our list to see what's happening. 1 Attack / unprotect- Black just took my Queen on d2 so I played 21 Rxd2 weakening the back rank, leaving the h1 Rook unprotected, strengthening the d file and the 2nd rank.

2 Checks and captures

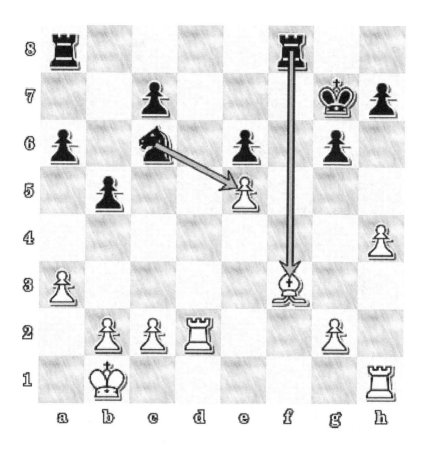

It`s Black`s move and it will take Black a few moves to put White in Check and I see two captures Nxe5 and Rxf3.

3 Undefended pieces

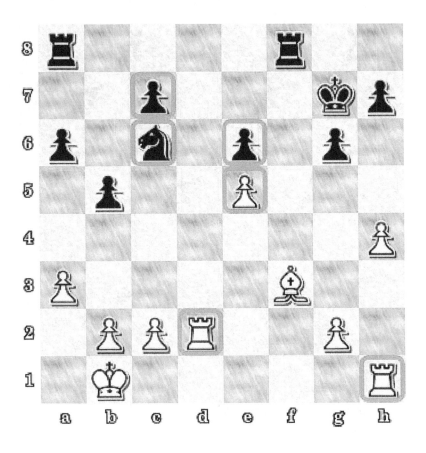

Black`s Knight on c6 and the pawns on c7 and e6 are undefended. White`s Rooks and pawn on e5 are undefended.

What's attacking / defending what

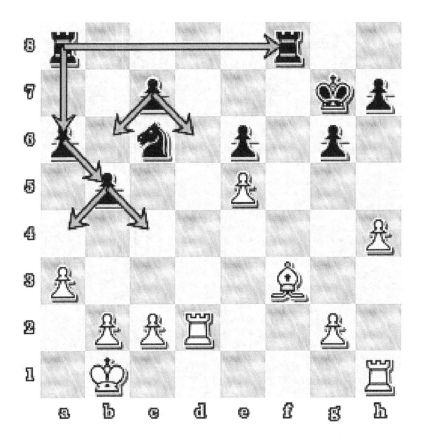

The a8 Rook is protecting the a file and the Rook on f8. The Queenside pawns are protecting a4, b6, b5, c4 and d6. The Knight is controlling 8 squares and if I used arrows it would obscure the board. The 8 squares are a7, a5, b4, d4, e5, e7, d8 and b8. The a5 and c5 squares are weak.

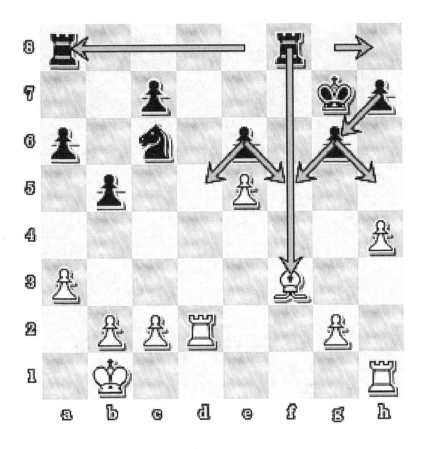

The f8 Rook is protecting the a8 Rook the back rank and attacking f3. The Kingside pawns are protecting d5, f5, g6 and h5. The King is protecting the 8 squares around it including the f8 Rook and two pawns, but again if I used arrows it would obscure the board. The f6 and h6 squares are weak.

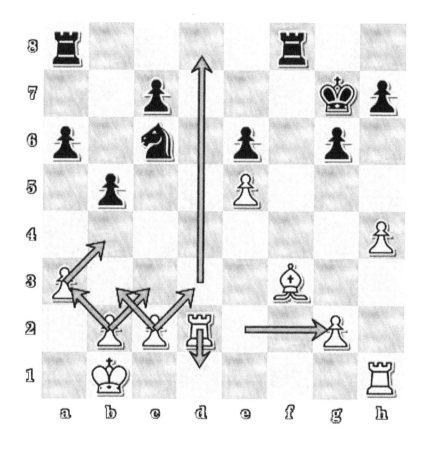

Now my pieces. The Queenside pawns are protecting a3, b3, b4, c3 and d3. The d2 Rook is protecting the d file and the 2nd rank. The King is protecting a1, a2, b2, c1 and c2.

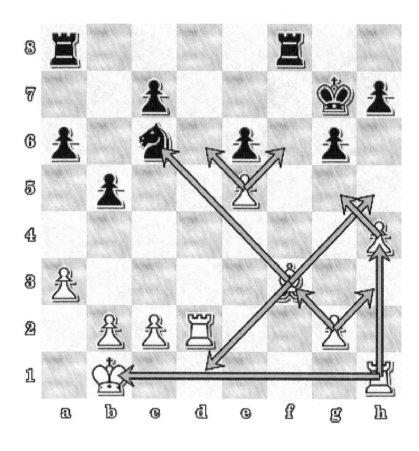

The Kingside pawns are protecting d6, f6, f3, h3 and g4. The Bishop is attacking the Knight and protecting the h1-a8 and d1-h5 diagonal. The h1 Rook is protecting the back rank and the h file.

5 Attack every piece

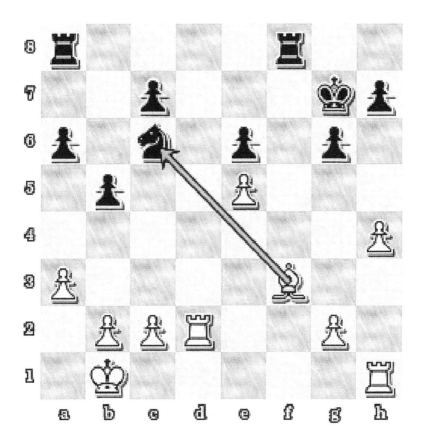

I'm attacking his Knight right now of course, but it`s not my turn. I don`t see a way to attack his Rooks for a few moves. He can save his Knight by moving the a8 Rook to d8 breaking the pin and attacking my d2 Rook which in the game is what he did.

6 Pins- We just identified the Knight on c6 being pinned to the Rook.

7 Best piece placement

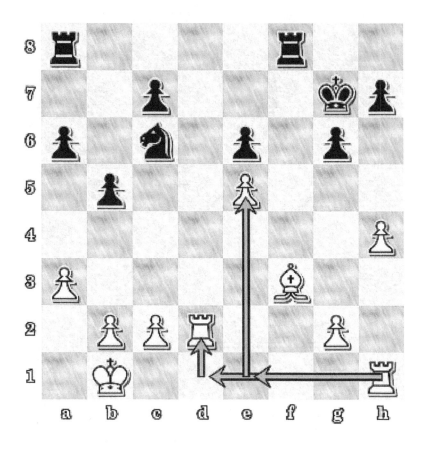

My worst placed piece is my h1 Rook. I would like to double
my Rooks on the d file or place it on the e file to protect e5 if I
must. I prefer the d1 option.

8 Moves pieces contact

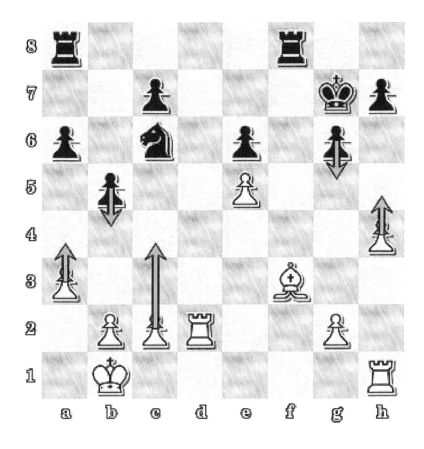

The pawn moves a4, c4, h5 for White and b4 and g4 for Black bring opposing units into contact.

21 ...Rd8

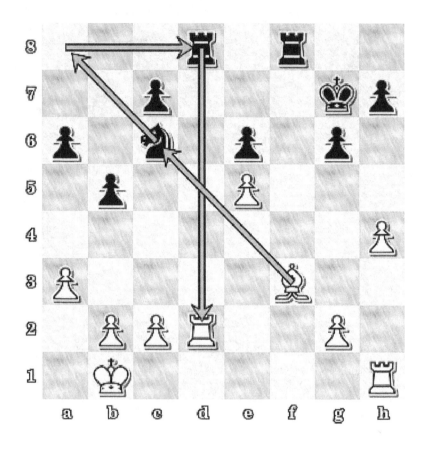

Weakening, the a file leaving a6 unprotected, strengthening the d file, breaking the pin on the c6 Knight and attacking the d2 Rook.

22 Rxd8

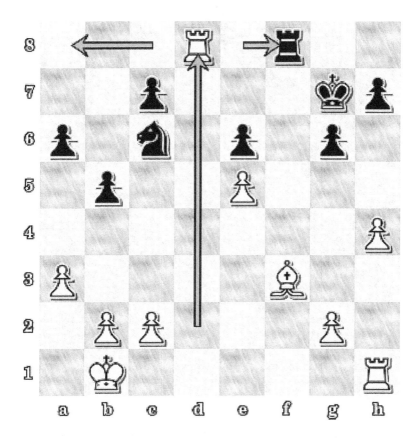

Weakening the 2nd rank, strengthening the 8th rank, capturing the d8 Rook and attacking the f8 Rook.

22 ...Nxd8

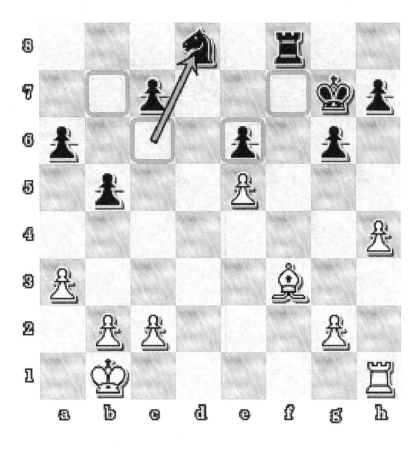

Weakening b8, a7, a5, b4, d4, e5, e7 and ironically d8, strengthening b7, c6, e6 and f7 and capturing the d8 Rook. In previous diagrams I used the arrows to show what the piece is attacking and strengthening and circles to show the squares that have been weakened, but a Knight move in the center often weakens 8 squares and strengthens 8 squares and there were so many arrows that it obscured the board. In diagrams with Knights I will use the arrows to show the move and what`s being attacked and circles to show the squares being strengthened and list the squares being weakened.

23 Rd1

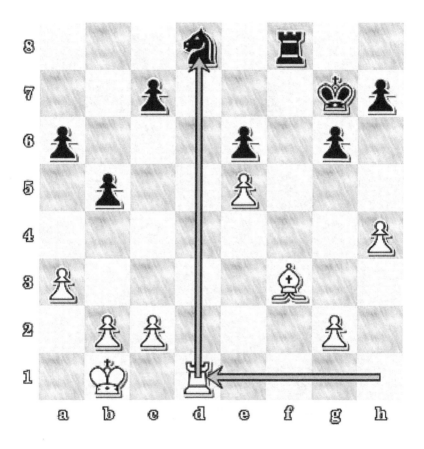

Weakening the h file leaving the h4 pawn unprotected, strengthening the d file and attacking the Knight on d8.

23 ...Nf7

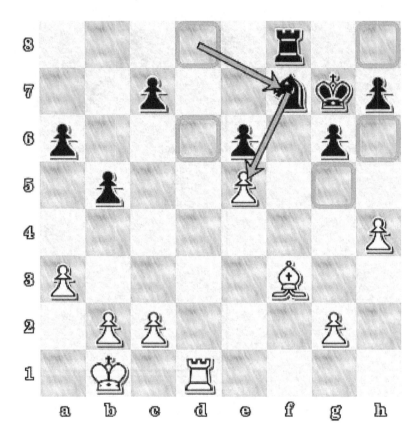

Weakening b7, c6, e6 and f7, strengthening d8, d6, e5, g5, h6 and h8 and attacking the e5 pawn.

24 Rd7

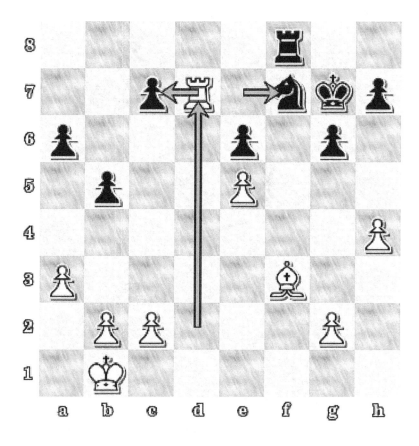

Weakening the 2nd rank, strengthening the 7th rank, attacking c7, pinning the f7 Knight and protecting e5.

24 ...c5

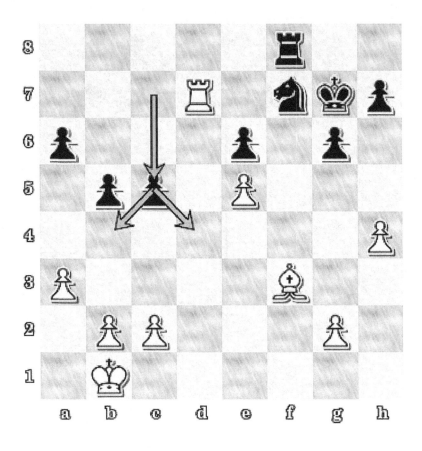

Weakening b6, b5, d6 and d5, strengthening b4 and d4 and saving the pawn.

25 Re7

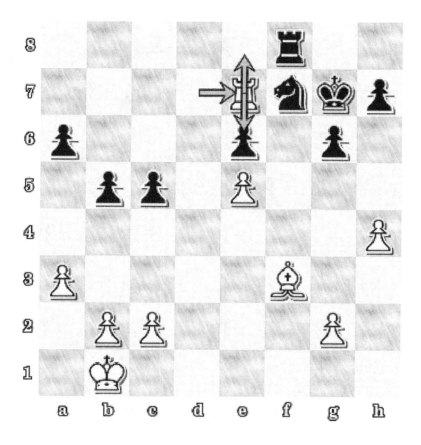

Weakening the d file, strengthening the e file and attacking the unprotected e6 pawn.

25 ...Rd8

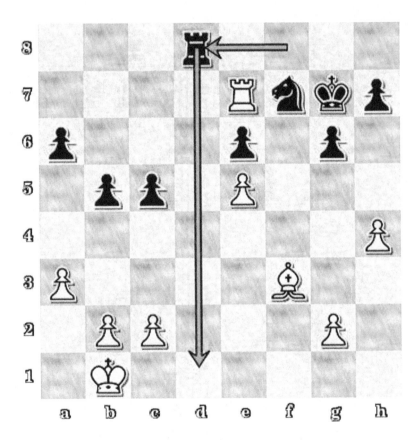

Weakening the f file, strengthening the d file and getting the Rook to the open file.

26 Rxe6

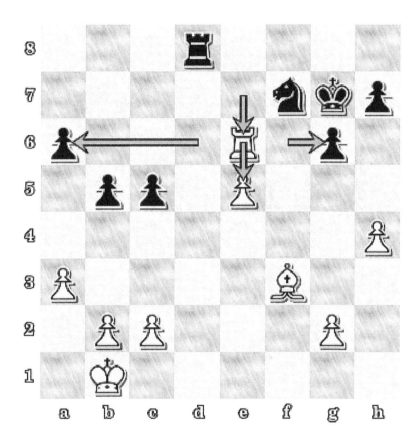

Weakening the 7th rank, strengthening the 6th rank, capturing the e6 pawn, attacking the pawn on a6, protecting the e5 pawn and giving up the pin on the f7 Knight.

26 ...a5

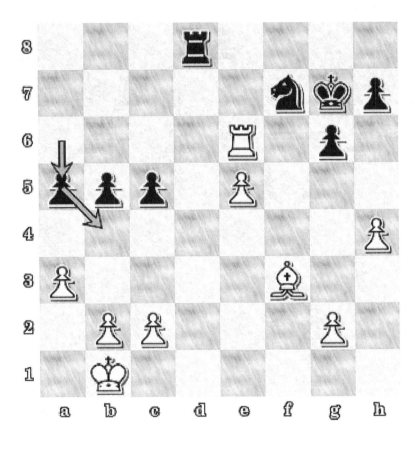

Weakening b5, strengthening b4 and moving the pawn to safety.

27 Re7

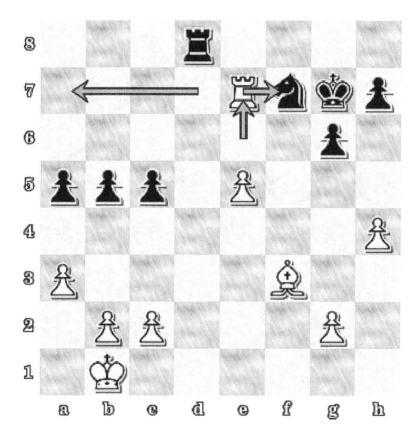

Weakening the 6th rank, strengthening the 7th rank and reestablishing the pin on the f7 Knight.

27 ...Rd4

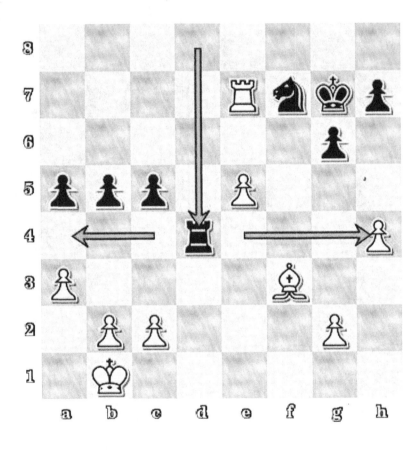

Weakening the 8th rank strengthening the 4th rank and attacking the pawn on h4. This was a mistake. I thought he would play Kf8 breaking the pin and attacking the Rook. He wanted to attack h4 and help his Queenside pawns down the board.

28 e6

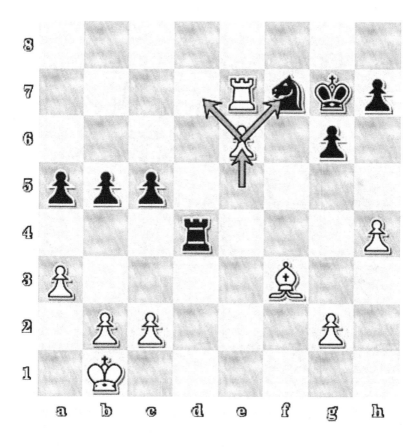

Weakening d6 and f6, strengthening d7 and attacking the pinned f7 Knight. Always try to break pins as soon as you can before you look for an attack.

28 ...Kf6

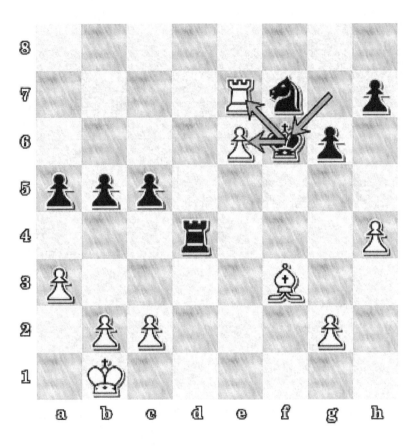

Weakening f8, g8, h8, h7and h6, strengthening e5, f5 and g5, (I`m not using arrows to show these squares as it obscures the King) and attacking the e7 Rook and e6 pawn.

29 Rxf7+

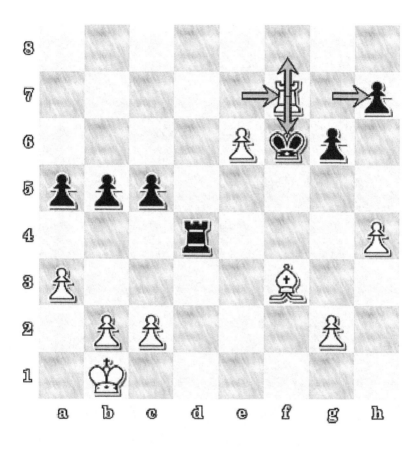

Weakening the e file leaving the e6 pawn unprotected, strengthening the f file, attacking the King and the h7 pawn.

29 ...Kxe6

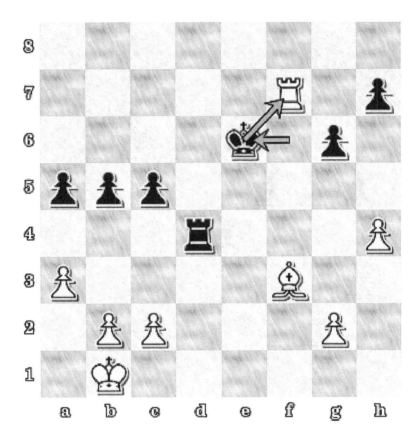

Weakening g7 and g5, strengthening d7, d6 and d5, capturing the e6 pawn and attacking the f7 Rook.

30 Rxh7

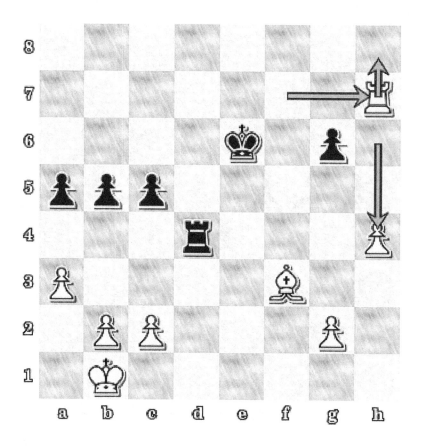

Weakening the f file, strengthening the h file and capturing the h7 pawn.

30 ...Kf6

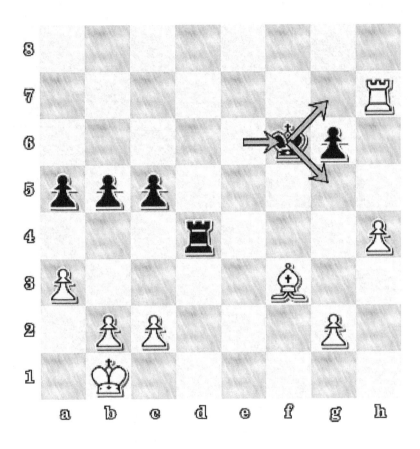

Weakening d7, d6 and d5, strengthening g7 and g5 and protecting the g6 pawn.

31 h5

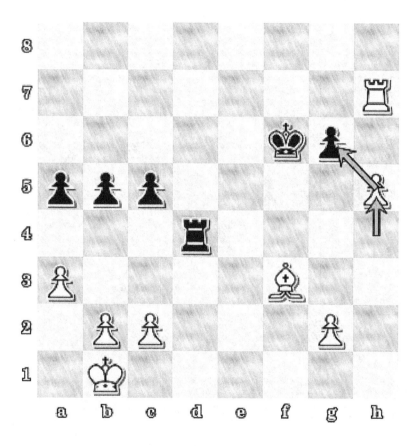

Weakening g5 and attacking the g6 pawn.

31 ...gxh5

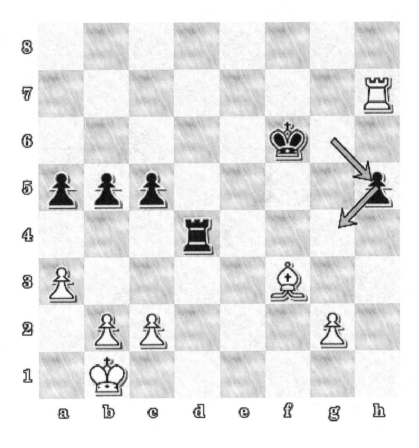

Weakening f5, strengthening g4 and capturing the h5 pawn.

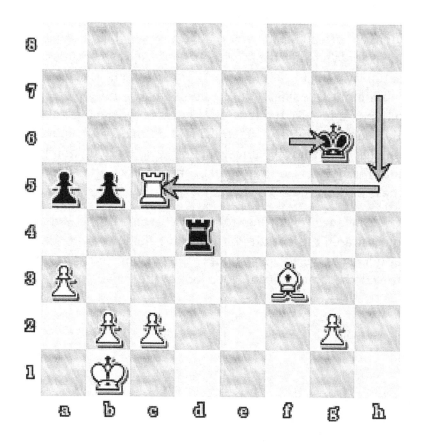

I played 32 Rxh5 winning the h5 pawn. My opponent, down a minor piece and realizing that a win was going to be difficult, just attacked the Rook and played 32 ...Kg6. I played 33 Rxc5 winning another pawn and my opponent resigned.

Using our 8 Step process we were again able to define the position and find reasonable moves without any grievous blunders. Let`s look at a game I played starting at move 1.

Another resource I should mention for finding Opening ideas is, of course the Internet. One day while looking for ideas for White against the French Defense I came across this setup by Gunjan Jani. He posts videos about various traps in different Openings. While I don`t think you should spend all your time just trying to set traps, (the Opening I spend the least amount of time studying) I do think you should be familiar with traps in various Openings so that you don`t fall into them. His videos are great fun and I like how when he makes a good move he always says "Bam!"

Since we`re starting from move 1 some of the Steps on our list aren`t relevant right away, but we do want to glance at our list as we go along, update the position and note when they do become relevant. Let`s look at the game.

1 e4

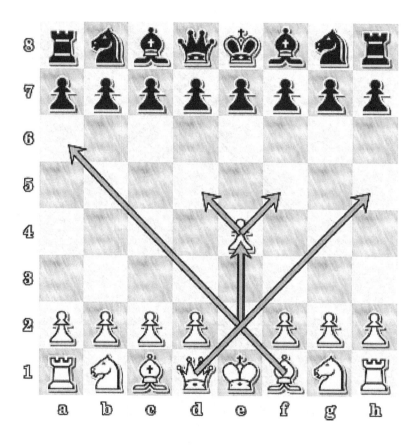

Weakening d3, d4, f3 and f4, strengthening d5 and f5 and opening the d1-h5 and f1-a6 diagonals.

1 ...e6

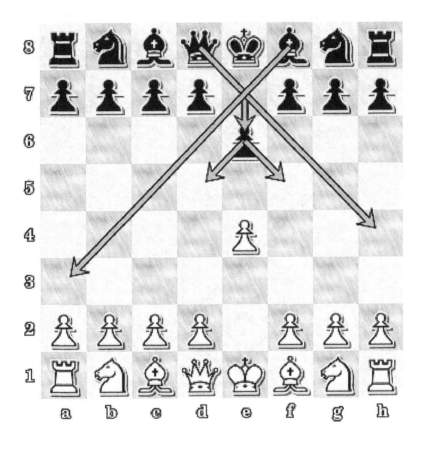

Weakening d6 and f6, strengthening d5 and f5 and opening
the d8-h4 and f8-a3 diagonals.

2 Nf3

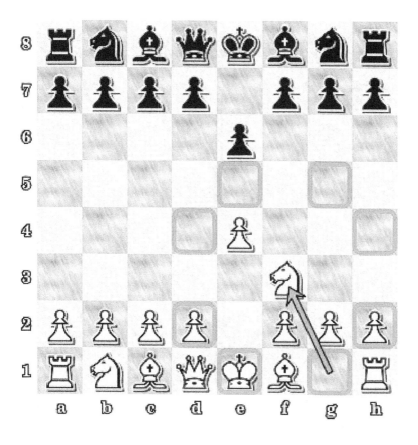

Weakening e2, f3 and h3, strengthening e1, d2, d4, e5, g5, h4, h2 and g1. The moves d5 and f5 both bring units into contact with e4. (Step 8)

2 d5

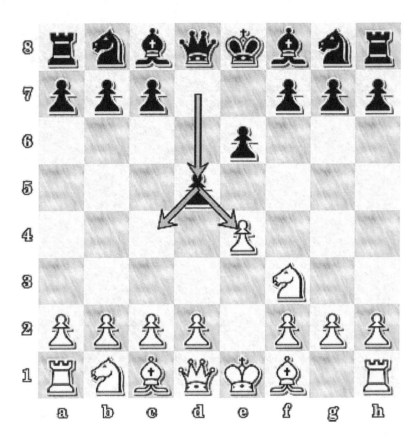

Weakening c6, c5, e6 and e5, strengthening c4 and e4, the e4 pawn is unprotected. There is a Check with Bb5. (Step 2) We want to note it, but it`s unviable for now.

3 Nc3

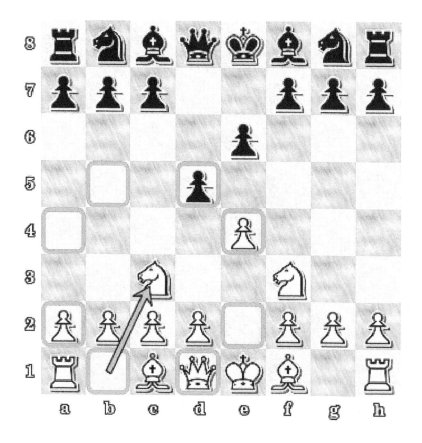

Weakening a3 and d2, strengthening a2, a4, b5, e4, e2, d1 and b1 and attacking the d5 pawn. The d5 pawn can reach the c3 Knight on the next move. (Step 8)

3 ...c5

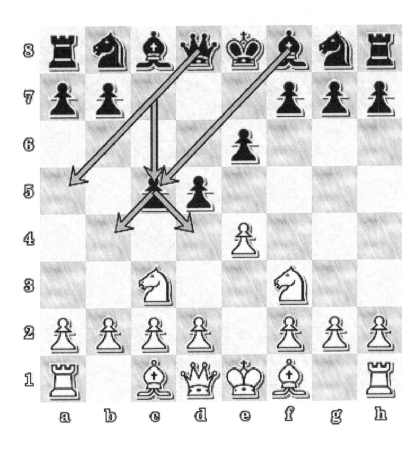

Weakening b6, b5, d5 and the d6 square is weak, strengthening b4 and d4, opening the d8-a5 diagonal for the Queen and blocking the f8-a3 diagonal for the Bishop which is protecting c5.

4 exd5

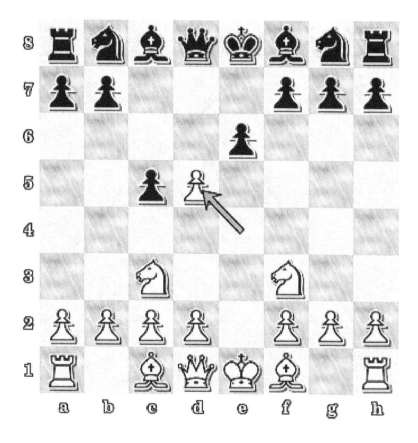

Weakening d5 and f5 and capturing the d5 pawn. The pawn on d5 is strengthening e6 and c6, but it won`t be around for long so I didn`t bother to add arrows.

4 ...exd5

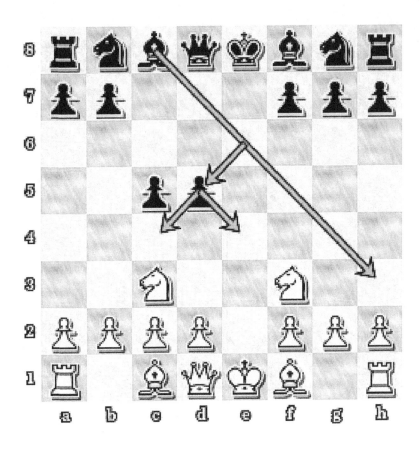

Weakening d5 and f5, strengthening c4 and e4 and capturing the d5 pawn. Opens the c8-h3 diagonal allowing the Bishop contact with the Knight (Step 8) and the e file is open for both sides. The move d4 contacts the Knight. (Step 8) Two Checks are possible, Bb5+ and Qd2+, the capture Nxd5 is unviable. (Step 2)

5 Bb5+

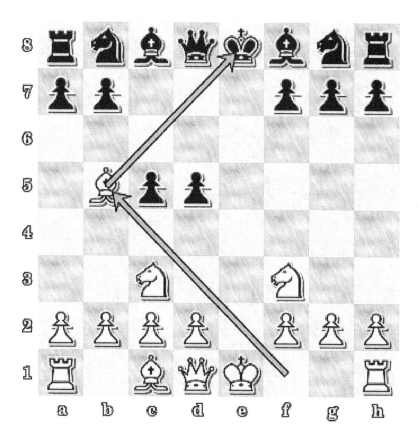

Weakening g2, strengthening the a4-e8 diagonal and Checking the King. The pawn push to a6 will bring the pawn and Bishop in contact. (Step 8)

5 ...Nc6

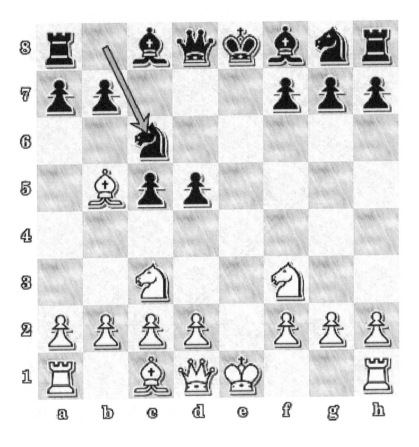

Weakening a6 and d7 and blocking the Check by the Bishop. Ordinarily a Knight on c6 strengthens 8 squares, but for the moment the Knight is pinned. (Step 6)

6 Qe2+

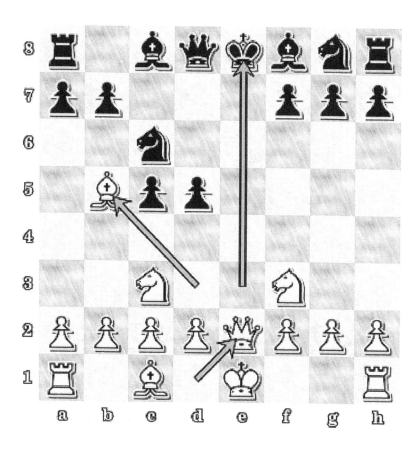

Weakening c2, strengthening the f1-a6 diagonal, the e file, protecting the Bishop (Step 4) and Checking the King. (Step 2)

6 ...Be7

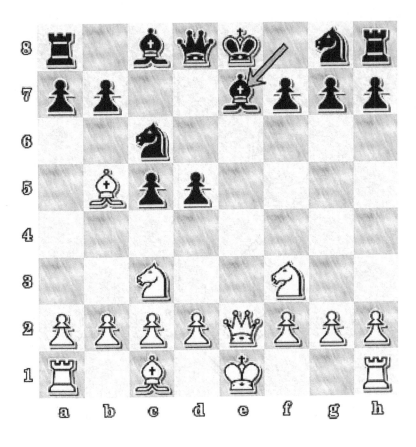

Weakening g7 and blocking the Check. The c5 pawn is unprotected and the d8-h4 diagonal is weakened because of the pin. (Step 6)

7 Ne5

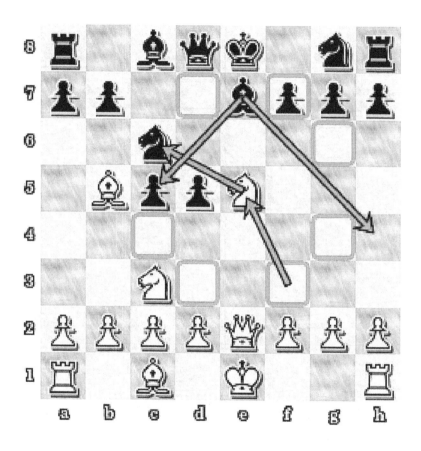

Weakening e1, d2, d4, e5, g5, h4, h2 and g1. Blocks the pin on the e7 Bishop strengthening the d8-h4 and f8-a3 diagonal for Black. Strengthening d3, c4, c6, d7, f7, g6, g4 and f3. Attacking the pinned Knight on c6.

7 ...Qd6

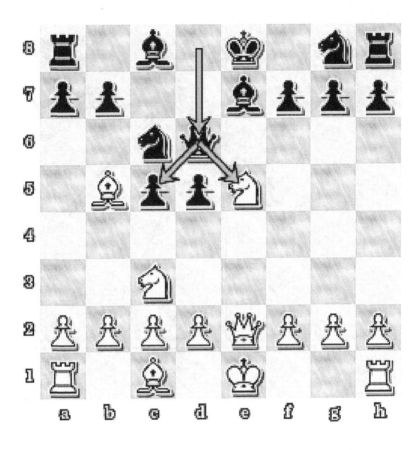

Weakens the back rank, the d8-a5 and d8-h4 diagonals, strengthens the 6th rank, c5 and attacks the Knight. The Queen is getting overworked. He wanted to protect the Knight on c6 and the d5 pawn. (Step 4) Protecting the Knight with the Bishop blocks the Queen`s protection of d5.

8 d4

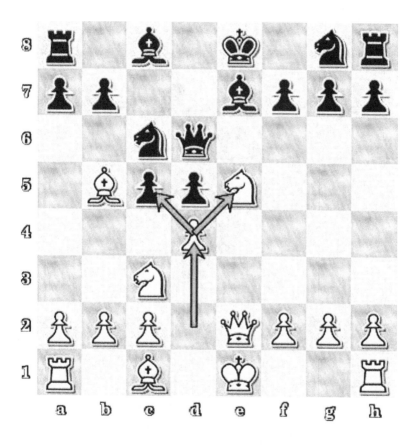

Weakening c3, c4, d3 and d4, strengthening c5 and protecting
the e5 Knight. Opens the c1-h6 diagonal for the c1 Bishop and
offering a pawn sacrifice.

8 ...cxd4

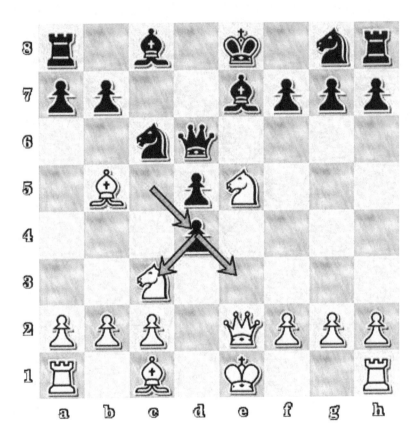

Weakening b4 and d4, strengthening e3, capturing the gambit pawn, isolating the d5 pawn, attacking the c3 Knight and opening the a3-f8 diagonal.

9 Bf4

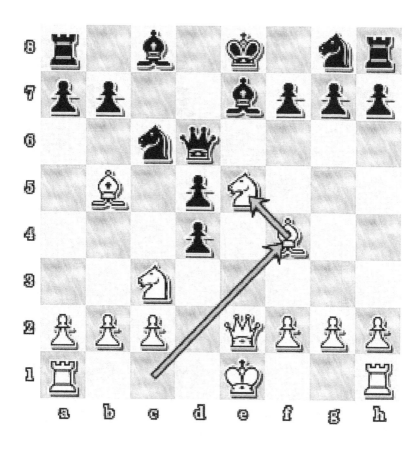

Weakening b2, strengthening the h2-b8 diagonal, protecting the e5 Knight, threatening a discovered attack against the Queen and offering the c3 Knight. Here my opponent thought for a while. He knew something was up, but the c3 Knight was just too tempting.

9 ...dxc3

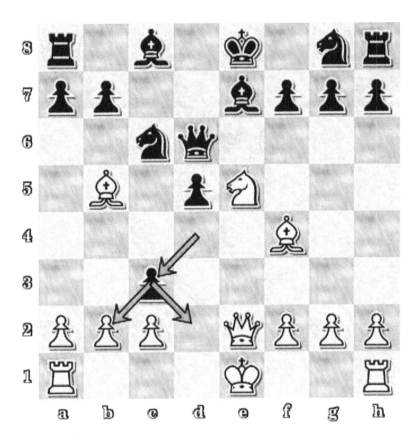

Weakening d3 and c3, strengthening b2 and d2 and capturing the c3 Knight. The c3 pawn is unprotected. (Step 3)

10 Nxc6

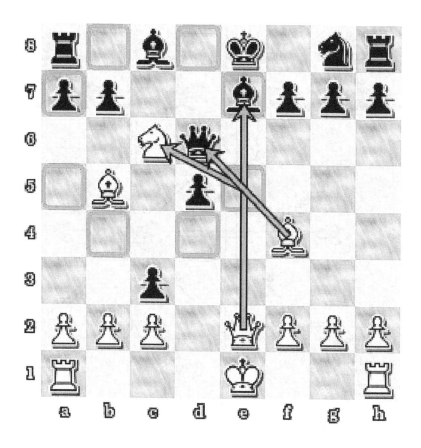

Weakening d3, c4, c6, d7, f7, g6, g4 and f3, strengthening b4, a5, a7, b8, d8, e7, e5 and d4, captures the c6 Knight, pins the e7 Bishop, (Step 6) opens a discovered attack against Black`s Queen, attacks the e7 Bishop and threatening a discovered Check with the b5 Bishop.

10 ...Qxf4

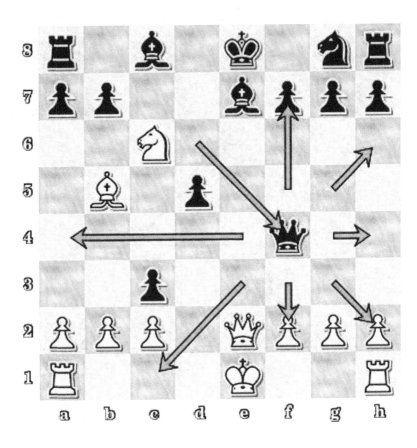

Weakening the d file, 6th rank, f8 -a3 diagonal, leaving the d5 pawn unprotected, strengthening the f file, the 4th rank, the c1-h6 diagonal, attacking the h2 pawn and threatening Check on d2.

11 Nxe7+

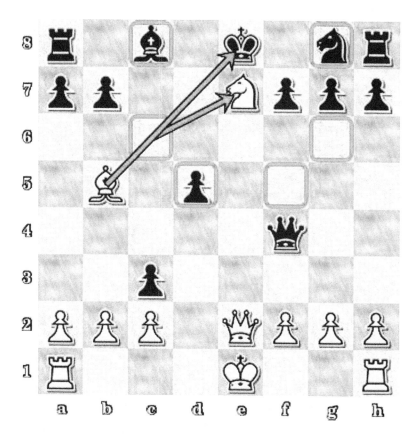

Weakening b4, a5, a7, b8, d8, e7, e5 and d4, strengthening c8, g8, g6, f5, d5 and c6, capturing the Bishop and uncovering a Check against Black`s King from the b5 Bishop.

11 ...Bd7

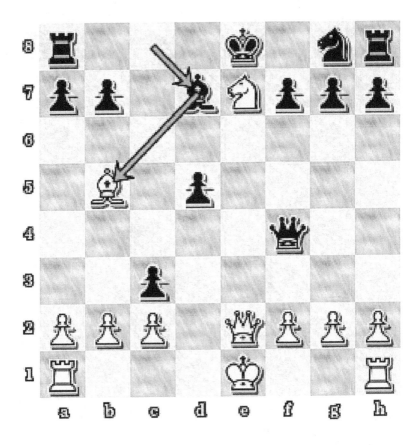

Weakening the c8-h3 diagonal due to the pin, leaving the b7 pawn unprotected, blocking the Check and attacking White's b5 Bishop. I thought he would play Kd8. Kf8 leads to Ng6+ f or hxg6 Qe8#

12 Nxd5+

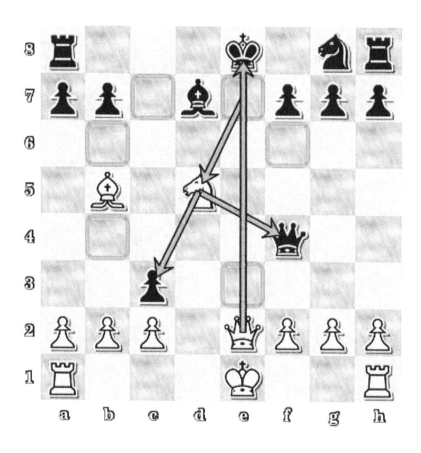

Weakening c8, g8, g6, f5, d5 and c6, strengthening c3, b4, b6, c7, e7, f6, f4 and d3, attacking Black`s Queen, c3 pawn and uncovering a Check against Black`s King.

12 ...Ne7 13 Qxe7#

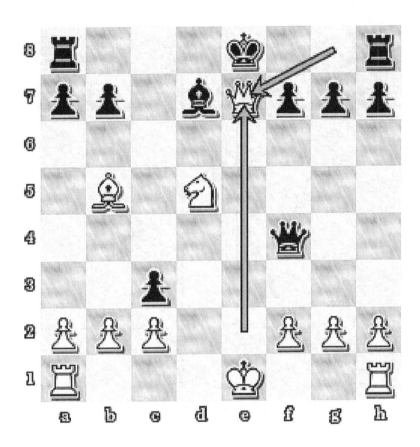

Here my opponent realized he was in Check and he was going to lose his Queen, but Bob's no quitter and he reflexively played Ne7 blocking the Check leading to Qxe7#. He had used a significant amount of time on his clock while I had used very little time because this Opening setup was in my catalog of games.

I hope this approach to improving at chess and finding better moves is helpful to anyone that reads this book. Is this how great chess players find their moves? I`m not sure, but how would I know? I live down here with mere mortals. It has helped me to think more systematically, find better moves and most importantly to stop making so many horrific blunders that plague players at our level.

I would love to hear from you. Please feel free to e mail me at jamesdemery@yahoo.com. Any feedback would be appreciated.

The diagrams I used in this book are from jinchess.com. If you would like to print out diagrams of your game positions check out this site.

Good luck with your chess!

Made in the USA
Las Vegas, NV
21 October 2023